Missions of Honor

Written by Donald J. Fitzgerald

-Dedication-

This book is about a special mission my friend and I worked on together for almost three years (and one I continue still on my own.) I was excited over the idea of putting a book together and sharing our many adventures with the rest of the world. When I put the first version of this book together, I was only twelve years old.

Before I begin sharing our *Missions of Honor* journey, I want to dedicate this very special project to the memory of my last grandfather, retired Army Chief Warrant Officer (CW3) William Marshall Fitzgerald, Sr. My grandfather was a Veteran who fought and flew in three combat-tours in the Vietnam War who then became a member of the Merchant Marines.

My grandfather was an extremely intelligent man and a big believer in advanced education. In fact, he'd earned several different college degrees during his lifetime in various subjects as well as having been both an airplane and helicopter pilot during the Vietnam War.

My Grandpa never sat still for long and was *always* looking at ways to increase his knowledge. Like I said, he was a very smart man. Sadly, just ten days before I officially became a teenager, my awesome grandfather passed away from an unexpected heart attack in Roundrock, Texas.

I brought up education because it seemed my Grandpa was *always* learning new things. It really was no surprise to me that when I asked him and Grandma if they wanted to take part in my Medal of Honor mission while visiting San Antonio in 2016, that they wanted to go. Grandpa had never heard about anybody walking through National Cemeteries (any cemeteries, actually) in search of Medal of Honor recipients. He walked right along with me, reading the research I had written and brought along about the men we were paying respects to. He really enjoyed being part of my mission.

I *always* loved going to Texas to visit my grandparents. Whenever we'd go to their house, we always did fun things. We'd sit together and play music with Grandpa or watch movies in the living room with big bowls of popcorn. As a matter of fact, Grandpa taught me how to use a metal detector on one of our visits. I always had fun and loved my Grandpa very much. When he died, it was not at all expected. Grandpa had always been a part of my life but suddenly, just before my birthday in 2017, he was gone. Grandpa died on Grandma's birthday, December 06th 2017. I'll never forget the date.

I dedicate this book to my Grandpa and thank him (and Grandma) for coming along with me on my honor missions in San Antonio. The last time I got to see Grandpa, me, him, and my dad took a road-trip to Bandera, Texas to visit the *War at Home Memorial*. (Another of my Mom's Marines from the 1/5 is a part of that memorial; Marine Sargent Brandon C. Ladner.) We had also stopped in Austin at the State Cemetery to visit American Sniper Chris Kyle's final resting place during that same trip. We paid respects to *many* heroes but for me, my grandpa was a hero, too. I thought it was great that he was interested in my project.

Before anybody thinks it was crazy that my parents and grandparents took me all over the country to visit different cemeteries, you really should read this book. There were many specific reasons why I did what I did, why I started this project with one of my elementary school classmate (and introducing a few other friends to take part in various missions.) These trips/missions were so much more than just about going to cemeteries. Even when the official mission was complete, and my friend didn't want to do this project any more, I kept learning about other Medal of Honor Recipients and continued traveling all over the country.

This is a book about my Medal of Honor Missions, why I invited my friend to help, why I created this project, and how it all started and how we (kind of) finished. It's with a lot of love and happiness that I look back at this lengthy journey that took about three years to complete and am proud that the last grandpa in my life chose to be part of it, too. *"Thank you, Grandpa."*

Our Missions of Honor turned into a project I wanted to share with people. It started out as literally a cut and pasted project of real pictures and stories that my mom encouraged me write out by hand (in cursive, by the way) to turning into this book that Mom helped me get published. *"Thanks, Mom."*

After beginning this project with my friend, I wanted to be sure to tell people I actually visited a lot more places than just the ones Derrick went with us to. My family tended to travel by car to a lot of different places, plus, I was busy trying to earn every single Merit Badge the Boy Scouts of America had to offer. So, in traveling to different Merit Badge events in surrounding states, we took regular car trips and turned them into opportunities to learn more about heroes who happened to be at rest along the way.

People who really had no idea about what we were doing or why would call our trips *'just looking for grave yards'* or ask, *"So, you guys going to visit more dead people?"* I think I can say this for both me and my friend that we learned a lot about the men (and one woman) who earned this nation's highest military honor: The Medal of Honor.

Even though I've called our mission complete, I know we could have continued it as a team for a very long time. It took three years to get to this point and we barely hit the tip of the Medal of Honor iceberg. The heroes we learned about and visited each went through a lot but only ever considered themselves and their actions as *'just doing their job'*. There aren't a lot of living Medal of Honor recip-ients left but my friend and I (and Mom, too) have had the opportunity to meet, greet, shake hands with, get autographs of and pictures with about thirty of those still with us today.

I officially began (and with my friend Derrick, temporarily paused) our mission in Scio, New York. Scio is the birthplace of Medal of Honor Recipient Marine Jason Dunham. Jason was the first Marine to receive a Medal of Honor since the Vietnam War. Jason Dunham had jumped on a grenade, saving the lives of fellow Marines. He did not survive. The sad fact is that he received his Medal after he passed away. Jason Dunham never knew he'd received the Medal of Honor.

I had the unexpected opportunity to eat lunch with his parents, Mr. and Mrs. Dunham at their home. While Mom and I were visiting Scio, we also stopped by the local post office which had been renamed in Jason's honor. (We'd visit Scio again in 2017 and take my friend Derrick with us when the town dedicated new road signs in Jason's name.)

Before Mom and I traveled up to Scio the first time though, she and I had already been on a special visit in Virginia at *Arlington National Cemetery's* Section 60. It was Memorial Day, 2014, and we had driven there to join a special Marine's family with many of his fellow Marine brothers and friends to pay our respects. Mom had just written and published a book the previous year about a young Marine named Lance Corporal David R. Baker called *From Yellow Ribbons to a Gold Star.*

I really didn't know too much about what the Medal of Honor was about until Mom explained everything to me and Derrick. You see, it was around the same time that schools were messing with their curriculums. I didn't know what a curriculum was either, until Mom explained it to me. She (and a ton of other parents all over the country) was not happy with the many changes that seemed to be happening but most especially was unhappy with the fact that kids were not being taught cursive writing any more. That was how my whole Medal of Honor project pretty much got started; cursive writing. (Who'd have thought, right?) Mom had Derrick and I write in cursive whenever we did research about anything for our project.

Over all, our mission became an adventure of a lifetime. We met so many nice people, (many of Mom's Veteran contacts) traveled to some great locations, and besides learning a lot, also put thousands of miles on the car. We went to many places all over Arkansas first and then we went to Nashville and Chattanooga, Tennessee then to Leavenworth, Kansas. We also hit Kentucky,

Indianapolis, Indiana, Cincinnati, Ohio and many places in Missouri, too. (I traveled as far away as San Antonio, Texas and Otisfield, Maine, too never mind the various other trips to Georgia, Tennessee, Ohio, New York, Arlington, Virginia and Pennsylvania.)

We learned about a famous WWI Veteran named Sargent York, the Veterans in the *Tomb of the Unknowns* at Arlington (Medal of Honor Recipients), as well as visiting the World War II Museum in New Orleans. On a separate trip later the same year, Mom took me to Kansas City to the World War I Museum. I wish Derrick could have gone with us, but I was on a Boy Scout Merit Badge trip that was taking place in northwestern Missouri that weekend and the museum was on our way.

I am only speaking for myself when I say this. *Both* my parents are Veterans of the United States Army. My grandpa, William Marshall Fitzgerald was a pilot in the Army during Vietnam and my mom's grandpa was a paratrooper in the Korean War. They are all Army Veterans.

I'm thinking about joining the Coast Guard myself when I get old enough because nobody in my family has ever served with them yet. (I plan on doing that after I earn my Eagle Scout rank with the Boy Scouts of America.) While researching all our Medal of Honor information, an interesting fact that I learned was that the Coast Guard has only had one MOH recipient. That's what got me to thinking…

I'm very proud of this project and have been glad that so many different people were able to share the mission with me over the years. I hope this book makes people want to learn more about the Medal of Honor. It did for me and even though this part of the mission is complete, this whole ordeal isn't over yet. It took us several years to accomplish this much. We may not have yet begun to touch the tip of the iceberg as far as paying our respects to so many heroes, but we sure have learned a lot about so many ordinary men who did extraordinary things.

-A Few Facts-

When I told Mom that I wanted to write a book about our MOH missions, she suggested I do a lot more reading and research about everyone than what I had already done. She said this was a very ambitious project for a young man and that I had better know my stuff when I put it all to paper. *"You're likely going to be put under a microscope by a lot of people,"* she said. I learned what she meant by that after our first year of doing this project. She also suggested I make my Medal of Honor project into something that nobody else had ever thought of doing.

> *"Don't just rewrite what other people have already written. Make your book something people would like to learn more about. Don't just collect other people's facts and create another book about heroes. Write about the things that you and Derrick specifically did and how you felt or how you and Grandpa or your dad or me..."*

Mom didn't have to finish that sentence because I already knew what she was talking about. She still had us plan and map out our trips and read up on information about the people we were going to be traveling to pay respects to, though. She said that was an im-portant part of the mission, to know why we were paying respects to so many people in so many different places.

So, this next stuff I write about is not just information copied out of somebody else's book. These are things I thought would help make other people better understand our Medal of Honor Missions. It's been so much more than just visiting dead people or going to different cemeteries around the country. People will either under-stand that or they won't.

I put a lot of pictures in this book and talk about many of the people my friend and I researched, learned and wrote about, but know this. This book does not show *every* single picture or tell about *every* man (and the one woman) we learned about who earned the Medal of Honor. Like I said before, there are already books and articles about every single one of these heroes as well as about the thousands of others. This book was a great personal project and so many neat things happened to us along the way. I wanted to share those stories, so I wrote a book for other people to read. I know I'm lucky for having my Mom and Dad able to help me and my friend do something like this. Not every kid gets to do this kind of stuff and not every parent can take the time.

The Medal of Honor was America's first combat medal. It's the *only* award that hangs on a ribbon that the person receiving it wears around his neck. It's illegal for any person who has not earned a MOH to wear one. If somebody ever claims that they are a recipient and you think it could be untrue, just look up their name on the computer to check. Besides that, if a person says that they are a recipient and they really aren't, that's called stolen valor.

The Medal of Honor was created in 1861 to recognize men who distinguished themselves "*conspicuously by gallantry and intrepidity*" in combat with an enemy of the United States. It is awarded for acts of valor above and beyond the call of duty and is an honor presented by the President of the United States. More than half of all Medals of Honor have been awarded posthumously (after the person has died). There have been over 3,450 awarded with there being just 19 men who received *two* Medals of Honor (double recipients). In 1990, Congress declared March 25 '*National Medal of Honor Day*.'

Many people will argue the award is officially called the *Congressional* Medal of Honor. That's not true. It is called *The Medal of Honor* and there are three versions of it, one for the Army, one for the Navy and one more for the Air Force. (The Navy, Marines, and Coast Guard all share a design.) Speaking of the Coast Guard, remember I said how the Coast Guard only had one recipient of the Medal of Honor? His name was Douglas Munroe and he earned his Medal for his actions at World War II's *Guadalcanal*. He sacrificed his own life so a bunch of Marines could get to safety. He lived just long enough to know that his actions saved a lot of men. Eight months after he did it, President Franklin Roosevelt awarded Mr. Munroe's Medal of Honor to his wife.

A young man named Willie Johnson was the youngest to have earned the Medal at the age of 11. He was 13 when he actually received it. In more recent history, the youngest recipient was twenty-years old when he earned his Medal at *Iwo Jima*.

Arkansas is the home of General Douglas MacArthur. He and his father Arthur (Arthur MacArthur) were for the longest time the *only* father and son in history to have each received the Medal of Honor. On January 16th, 2001 that changed. Theodore Roosevelt received a MOH for his actions (from over 100 years prior) at *San Juan Hill* in Cuba. His son Theodore Jr. received the honor as well, for his own actions on *Utah Beach* during World War II. (By the way, the honor has also been given to five sets of brothers.)

This is where I had permission from my mom to use one of her stories. She's a writer, a Veteran's advocate and is *always* writing stuff about her fellow Veterans. Thanks, Mom, for letting me use this to explain things.

—

Ft. Smith, Arkansas: A Story of Respect and Patriotism From an Unlikely Source
TM Fitzgerald
October 2014

The year was 2012, the month of April and the place? Fort Smith National Cemetery, Fort Smith Arkansas. The intent? Well, the intent could very easily have been considered more *preparation* for a much-anticipated visit to yet another National Cemetery planned the following month: a very special Memorial Day event at Arlington.

There was a Mama (whom herself was a Veteran of the United States Military) and her son; a very civic-minded (and musically accomplished) young man who traveled; *a lot*. The Fates found this mother and child, whom together had been visiting family in Fort Smith readying for their return journey home. To travel was always a *journey* with the two of them because Mam never traveled the straight-line home. *"Turn left?"* She would challenge the animated GPS that was frantically informing her to make the next left turn they were approaching. *"How about we turn right instead? Sometimes you have to take the road less traveled."* The route they traveled that day took them past the Fort Smith National Cemetery, a place where, despite having no family members at rest there, the two had visited together quite regularly.

"It's about paying respect," Mama told her son on a previous trip "-and teaching *you* why respect matters."

"Yes Ma'am."

That particular afternoon with the front gates of the cemetery in sight, Mama had decided to take her son on a sort of practice run for what they were planning to do at Arlington the following month on Memorial Day. This Mama was in the process of compiling the biography of a young Marine who had been killed in action in Afghanistan in October 2009 just 19 days after his birthday.

Mama and her son were going to be traveling to Arlington, Virginia to meet with that Marine's family (as well as a number of his Marine brothers and Navy Devil Docs) at his grave in Section 60. As far as stopping at the Fort Smith Cemetery, she did not have to suggest it. Her little boy was one-step ahead of her. In a serious, and oh so solemn little voice he said, "Mom, let's go pay some respects."

As per their regular routine, Mama approached the front gates and drove slowly through the distinct cemetery entrance. She paused at the plaque affixed to the brick wall displaying the Gettysburg Address.

"Tell me who gave that speech?" She prompted. This was their routine, as many of their trips took them to National Cemeteries and not just private ones.

"Abe Lincoln." Her son reached over to the radio. "We should turn this off, Mom." Mama nodded approvingly as her son unbuckled his seat belt and sat up on his knees for a better view out the windshield. "You know; we should go there sometime; Gettysburg. Can we? After Washington and Arlington, I mean?"

"Sure. That sounds like a really good idea, going to Gettysburg." (And we did, by the way. Several times, actually.) She eased their vehicle to the right, driving slowly on the narrow lane situated among meticulously aligned rows of white, marble markers.

"It's on the way to where we're eventually going, anyway."

"Remember. Say all their names out loud. You never know when the last time anybody said them." The little boy remembered verbatim the instructions conveyed to him by a Gold Star Mother named Laurie Holt (the mother of the Marine whose biography his mother was compiling) the previous year when he and his Mama set off on their first mission (of many) to Arlington.

As they made their way through the Ft. Smith National Cemetery, Mama talked her son through mini-history lessons, explaining the various wars and conflicts in which so many men had died. It was the little boy who first noticed a peculiarity among some of those stones. In the farthest corner of the front section of the cemetery, were graves situated among ones dating back to the Civil War. The unusual thing the child had taken notice of was the fact many of those particular markers held no dates, no names; simply "Unknown Soldier."

"Mom. Look at that one." The boy pointed out the windshield and read the stone. "Two Unknown US Soldiers 1154." He waited for her to respond. "There're *two* soldiers buried in that grave. And two over there-" His pint-sized voice trailed off as he fell deep into thought. As his Mama turned left and slowly began making their way to the newer part of the cemetery, the little boy spoke up again. "Mom, this sure is a sad place but you know, it's kind of a happy one too."

Giving her son her full attention, Mama stopped and placed their vehicle into park. Genuinely curious, she turned to face him and asked him to explain what he meant by his remark.

"Well, it's sad here because all these people died. It's sad because those people over there, those Unknown Soldiers, nobody knew who they were but it's happy here, too though because all these people," he pointed to a group of graves beside their vehicle "-all *their* moms and dads know where they are. They came home. Their parents know that their boys are buried here in Fort Smith, Arkansas but those guys," he pointed back to the Unknowns "-their moms never knew where their babies ended up. Probably nobody comes to visit or pay them respects."

Mama sat there reflecting the very wise words her little boy had just shared. She started the vehicle and shifted into drive. "That's all quite true, boy. Quite true."

"Mom!" Her son suddenly exclaimed.

Instinctively, Mama tapped the breaks. "What?"

"We don't have any people here, do we? I mean, none of these guys are our people, right?" The little boy looked out the windshield, curiously studying the rows of stones surrounding them.

"No sir, we sure don't. Not blood wise, anyway. But you know, in all reality Kiddo, these are *all* our people. These are Veterans and their families. These are all people who fought for our country. So even though they aren't related to us, they are *all* our people."

Satisfied with his Mama's answer, the boy sat silent in thought once more. Mama slowly drove along the rows, windows down, softly speaking each name out loud as they passed.

"Mom!" Her son once again blurted with a sense of urgency. Once again, Mama instinctively tapped the breaks.

"Boy! You have *got* to stop doing that!" She smiled at the little boy seated beside her. "What now?"

"We need to get one." Excitedly, he sat back up on his knees.

"Not to take home or anything, but we don't have any people here, right? None of these are our guys." He looked at his mom with a serious little face. "Not by blood, anyway."

"So, what do you mean *'we should get one'*? What are you talking about?" She asked again. By this time, Mama had stopped and placed the vehicle in park. Turning off the engine, she looked at her little boy who was already opening his door.

"We should adopt somebody. That way, whenever we come here, we'll have somebody in specific to respect. We can still pay respects to everybody else too, but right now when anybody asks us why we stop here or who we come to see, we don't have anybody. So, let's pick out somebody. Then that will be our guy to visit when we come to respect everybody else."

Mama couldn't fight her son's logic. "OK then. Let's walk around and see who draws us to them." She suggested, but her boy had already started walking purposefully, respectfully down the row of gleaming white marble markers adjacent to their truck. She stood beside the vehicle watching her child respectfully touch the top of each stone he passed. She heard him speak each name as it was etched in the stone and heard him as he worked his way with some effort through ranks and other unfamiliar abbreviations he encountered.

"This one, Mom. I think we should adopt this one." Mama walked up behind her son who was pointing to a stone they must have passed a dozen times on previous visits.

"Sam Rodger Brown." Mama read aloud. "Good name for a Marine." She wasn't surprised by her son's choice. After all, she was working on the biography of the young Marine who had been killed in Afghanistan in 2009, a young man who was killed just nineteen days following his birthday.

"We'll look up stats for Sam before we come back, find out what we can about him just like he was our guy, okay?" Mama looked at her little boy who had taken a knee and was touching the top of Sam Brown's marker. "He was in World War II." The little boy looked at the stone and traced Sam's name. "You know, they called the guys who fought in that one '*The Greatest Generation.*'"

Caught by surprise, Mom asked her son. "How do you know about *The Greatest Generation*?"

The little boy looked up at his Mama and smiled the biggest smile. "Don't you remember, Mom? *You* told me."

A long trip still ahead of them, Mama told her little boy, "Let's jot down Sam's information and we'll look him up when we get home. We have to get going."

"Wait, Mom." The little boy said. "Can I play him a song?" The little boy was already pulling his violin case from the truck.

"Of course you do. Play him the songs you're going to play next month in Arlington."

The little boy proceeded to play the most beautiful renditions of '*Amazing Grace*' and '*Nearer My God to Thee*' to the newest member of his family, a World War II era Marine named Sam Rodger Brown.

"They played that song on the Titanic, Mom. You think Sam knew it?"

"I'm going to guess he did, boy."

Mama and son safely returned home and unpacked. The little boy immediately took Sam Brown's information and put it in their den by the computer.

"So you don't forget, Mom."

"So *WE* don't forget." She smiled.

Mama and son soon grew busy preparing for their long drive to Washington, DC and Arlington, Virginia. "And Gettysburg, too Mom. Don't forget. You said."

"I said. I know."

It wasn't until *after* they had returned from their trip, their specific mission to Arlington (and various other places) complete that mother and son began researching information about the Marine named Sam Rodger Brown. The information they learned and eventually were given to assume surprised them.

"That little stone sure didn't tell us all this about Sam, did it?"

"No Ma'am. It sure didn't."

Sam Rodger Brown
Our United States Marine

Using various sources, Mama and her son learned a lot about the man they'd so randomly chosen to 'adopt' at the Fort Smith National Cemetery. As it turned out, Sam Brown was not only a Marine but also an American Indian; a Seminole born on January 10th, 1921 in Seminole County, Bowlegs Oklahoma. Sam Brown died July 01st, 2004 (the same year the little boy who decided to 'adopt' him would be born five months later.) Sam was also a member of the *Achena Indian Presbyterian Church* of Maud, Okla-homa, and a member of *Disabled American Veterans*.

Sam Brown had served in the United States Marines from October 1940 through December 1946 and was a platoon sergeant in *Carlson's Second Marine Raiders Battalion*, serving in the Pacific. Brown was the recipient of two Purple Hearts; one received on Makin Island (now known as Bataritari Island) and one on Guadalcanal with a Gold Star.

According to sources the boy and his Mama had not confirmed, Sam Brown's father was a man named Harry Ross Brown. Harry was born in the Seminole Nation, son of Elisha Brown, founder of the Oklahoma town Wewoka. Sam's mother Annie was the daughter of a Creek Indian Minister named Dorsey Fife, founder of *Achena Indian Church*.

The little boy and his Mama soon discovered Sam Brown had a number of brothers and sisters. His sister Betty had been run over and killed by a drunk driver (1913-1930), a brother Harry, who was buried in Houston Texas National Cemetery, (1915-1983), another sister, Mary Lilly Brown Harkins (1922-2007) and one more brother named Benjamin Alan, a WWII Army Air Force sergeant who, like his brother Sam was also a Purple Heart Recipient (1924-2000).

Sam Brown's grave marker indicated that he was a platoon sergeant so the little boy and his mother (who, by the way was an Army Veteran) looked up information with help from Google. This is what they found. (A great portion of the remainder of this story was compiled from facts found on popular search engines. Information about Sam Rodger Brown could not be 100% verified at the time of this writing due to the fact the majority of his family is deceased and there was to date no response from a daughter still living.)

The designation of platoon sergeant in the Marines is a duty position, not a regular rank. The platoon sergeant is more like an assistant or consultant to the actual platoon leader who has the responsibility of training and caring for his Marines. The platoon sergeant helps the commander train the platoon leader, so as such, he has enormous influence on how that young officer will perceive NCOs for the rest of his career.

A platoon sergeant will take charge of a platoon in absence of the platoon leader. (In the USMC, the billet of platoon sergeant is usually held by a Staff

Sergeant (E-6). The rank of Platoon Sergeant was officially authorized in 1929.) Today, the platoon sergeant oversees taking care of the Marines and the platoon's operational control while advising the platoon commander.

The civic-minded little boy did not know, but he was about to get an unexpected and surprising history lesson. During the process of researching Sam Brown, the little boy and his mother learned Sam had served on the island of Makin. (In fact, Sam received one of his purple hearts here.) Makin is the name of a chain of islands located in the Pacific Ocean island nation of Kiribati. It's the northernmost of the Gilbert Islands and of the five small islands that comprise Makin, only Makin and Kiebu are permanently inhabited.

On December 10, 1941, just three days following the attack on Pearl Harbor, Japan occupied Makin. The U.S. invaded the island in the Pacific campaign of World War II called appropriately enough, *The Battle of Makin* which lasted from November 20th to November 24th, 1943.

However, on August 17th of 1942, 211 Marines of the 2nd Marine Raider Battalion (of which this Marine, Sam Brown was a part of) under command of the famous Colonel Evans Carlson and Captain James Roosevelt (Theodore Roosevelts' son) landed on Makin from the submarines USS Nautilus and the Argonaut.

The Japanese garrison had only posted between 80 and 160 men on the Makin. The Marine Raiders killed at least 83 of them, annihilated the garrison, and destroyed installations suffering all while suffering a personal loss of just 21 with nine men captured. (The Japanese moved those nine prisoners to Kwajalein Atoll (Marshall Islands) where they were later executed.)

Wikipedia revealed that the whole objective of the Makin Island Raid was to confuse the Japanese about U.S. intentions in the Pacific. Instead, it had the unintended effect of alerting the Japanese of the strategic importance of the Gilbert Islands that led to their further reinforcement and fortification.

After Carlson's Raid, the Japanese reinforced the Gilberts, which until that time, had been left lightly guarded. In August of 1942, Makin was garrisoned with only a single company of the 5th Special Base Force. However, while the Japanese were building up defenses in the Gilberts, American forces were making plans to retake the islands.

"Then-Lieutenant Colonel Merritt A. Edson and almost 5,000 Marine Corps Raiders of World War II were legend in the South Pacific. Organized in January 1942 (and disbanded just two years later) the Raider battalions were developed as a Marine Corps special mission force, based on the success of the British commandos and Chinese guerrillas operating in northern China." (Wikipedia).

The Raiders (considered the predecessors of today's Marine Corps special operations forces) were *"established as amphibious light infantry meant to land and operate behind enemy lines. The Marine Raiders are lightly armed and intensely trained. Their mission: to spearhead larger, amphibious landings on beaches thought to be inaccessible, conduct raids requiring surprise and high speed, and to operate as guerrilla units for lengthy periods behind enemy lines."* (Wikipedia).

As far as learning all they could about their Marine, the little boy continued searching and reading through various online media. Here is the rest of what they discovered as posted on Wikipedia:

The Makin Raid in August 1942 by the 2nd Marine Raiders Battalion: Carlson's Raiders were one of the most famous Special Operations missions of World War II. Twenty-three men were awarded the Navy Cross, five posthumously, and one Marine, Sgt. Clyde Thomason, would be the first enlisted man to receive (posthumously) the medal.

Ten days later, a force of 221 men from the second Raider Battalion, Carlson's Raiders (named for its commanding officer, Lieutenant Colonel Evans F. Carlson) landed off two submarines on Butaritari Island, Makin Atoll. The raid was successful in that it inflicted heavy damage and forced the Japanese to divert troops from Guadalcanal. Edson and his Raiders, in conjunction with the Marines 1st Parachute Battalion, left their mark on the Guadalcanal campaign during the night of Sept. 13|14. The intense and vicious close quarters fight became known as the Battle of Edson's Ridge or Bloody Ridge Edson was among those decorated for heroism and received the Medal of Honor.

Refitted, rested and rearmed, the 2nd Raiders, again led by Carlson, landed on a remote Guadalcanal beach and conducted their famous operation Thirty Days Behind the Lines which took place November 04th to December 04th.

The Guadalcanal Campaign (also known as the Battle of Guadalcanal, codenamed Operation Watchtower) was a campaign fought between August 07th, 1942 and February 09th, 1943 on and around the island of Guadalcanal in the Pacific theatre of World War II. It was the first major offensive by Allied forces against the Empire of Japan. Guadalcanal marked the beginning of offensive operations that resulted in Japan's surrender and the end of World War II.

The preceding information about Sam Rodger Brown and associated elements was gathered out of the fact a little boy and his Mama decided to stop and pay respects to Unknown, unrelated soldiers and Marines interred in one of this country's National Cemeteries. Definitely not the expected result of any *Mom and Me* road trips your average little boy takes on an early summer afternoon.

"Are any of these people ours, Mom?"

"They *all* are."

———

-And Finally: The Beginning-

It was March 25th of 2015 (Medal of Honor Day) that my friend and I officially started working on our Missions of Honor together. At first, we were just going to travel all over Arkansas and Western Tennessee. When I shared this with my mom though, she said the whole idea really had already started a few years before when she and I visited Arlington for her Marine, David Baker. She said I could add some of her stories to this book to better explain how she ended up taking Derrick and I to so many different states and places in search of these heroes. (Derricks' Mom and Dad let *my* Mom borrow Derrick all the time,)

We started the Arkansas part of this project as we were on our way to Harrison, Arkansas for a fiddler's convention. (I have been playing the violin/fiddle since I was three years old and many times would play hymns to our heroes in respect.) The first person we visited was Maurice 'Footsie' Britt. Besides being a Medal of Honor recipient, Mr. Britt had also been a professional football player, famous for his size fourteen feet.

After spending some time in Little Rock, we headed farther north to a town named Harrison, Arkansas which was the birthplace of *another* Medal of Honor recipient named Jack Williams. We were also going to Springfield, Missouri as well since we were already traveling that far north. (It wouldn't be the farthest north we'd travel for this project though.) Like I said earlier, when we first started our mission, we'd only thought about a very small area to travel. Even though Derrick went with me to a lot of places, there were still a whole lot more he *didn't* go.

———

Maurice L. Britt

Me and Derrick in Springfield, MO

We learned a lot about so many different Medal of Honor recipients. I could write a little bit about each of them but that made me think about what Mom said about writing what other people had already written. Instead, this book is more about my own journey and what Derrick and I learned, did, and saw.

Even though we officially hit the one-year mark the following March, (Medal of Honor Day) Mom found another event for Derrick and I to attend in Gainesville, Texas where we got to watch a huge parade and then met almost thirty of our living heroes. It was an awesome way to end our mission. Little did we know though, that Gainesville *still* wasn't going to be the end.

———

-Douglas MacArthur-

One of the very first places we went to visit that wasn't a cemetery was in Little Rock, Arkansas. It was the MacArthur Museum of Military History, a national landmark built in 1840. Originally, this place was where gunpowder, ammunition, and cannons were stored. It had eventually been turned into Officer's Quarters and was where Douglas MacArthur was born.

When Douglas MacArthur first became a general in the United States Army, he was the youngest to do so at the age of 37. MacArthur eventually became a famous five-star general who was also famous for promising his troops, *"I shall return."* He is also known for saying, *"Old soldiers never die. They just fade away."*

It was while we were in Little Rock we first saw a real Medal of Honor. It was General MacArthur's. We would learn later that he and his father, Arthur MacArthur were the first father and son recipients of the Medal. They were the only ones for a long time and then the Roosevelts became the second set.

———

-Jason Dunham, United States Marine-

Born on the same day as the United States Marine Corps birthday (November 10th) Jason Dunham was a regular kind of guy that everybody loved. He played sports in his high school in Scio, New York and was the kind of person that other people called a natural-born leader.

When Mom and I went on our first trip to Arlington, Virginia for her Marine, Lance Corporal David Raymond Baker, we also traveled further north to Upstate, New York. Mom had researched information on a Medal of Honor Recipient at rest in a private cemetery there. His name was Jason Lee Dunham and he was a United States Marine.

Since we had not really started our Missions of Honor project, this trip was kind of the real beginning to all of that. Mom is a writer and had already put together an article, so I asked her if I could borrow some of that article to use in my book to help explain the beginnings of our Missions.

Two Dates, a Dash and One United States Marine
By: TM Fitzgerald

John 15:13 *"Greater love hath no man than this that he would lay down his life for his friends."*

Memorial Day Weekend, 2012. The journey began in the throes of an official call of duty at one of this Nation's most hallowed grounds: *Arlington National Cemetery*, a trip that reflected the continuation of a mission promised to a Gold Star mother the preceding year. Tending to the task for a very specific young Marine interred in Arlington, a veteran and her son eventually set themselves on a more northerly course to take holiday with family in Upstate New York. (The designation "Upstate New York" is one that must specifically be made to differentiate between the likes of Manhattan, Brooklyn or the

Bronx and the vast expanses of farm country located further north. New York is definitely *not* all highways and skyscrapers.)

The Veteran and her son were following an itinerary they had pieced together jointly: destination? Elmira, New York. About an hour north of Elmira was another town on their itinerary: Scio. Mother and son had completed their earlier task in Arlington, Virginia just days before and had planned to complete a similar mission in the sleepy, Upstate town of Scio, honoring and paying their respects to another young Marine; Medal of Honor Recipient Corporal Jason Lee Dunham.

If you place 367 people in the same room, the statistical odds of at least two people in that room having the same birthday is naturally a given. However, what of the probability of any people in that room being a Marine who shares a birthday with the United States Marine Corps?

For most people, November 10th, 314th day of the year, is simply another day. To a select group, this day means much more. It is the Marine Corps Birthday, but this particular date is something else as well. It is also the birthdate of Corporal Jason Dunham, a Marine who gave his life in service to his country April

22, 2004. This is a story about the line between the dates on his grave, an unexpected tale about a major portion of this Marine's dash.

Born and raised in Scio, New York, Dunham was a machine-gunner serving with the 3/7 1st Division I Marine Expeditionary Force in Al Ambar Province, Iraq when his battalion commander's convoy was ambushed. The course of that ambush found Corporal Dunham and his team patrolling a vehicle checkpoint, searching vehicles for weapons. From one of those vehicles, an Iraqi insurgent jumped and attacked Dunham. It was while wrestling him to the ground that Dunham observed the insurgent release a grenade, pin pulled. The young Marine immediately alerted his men of the threat. Without hesitation, Corporal Dunham jumped on the grenade, covering it with his helmet and smothering it with his body, shielding his fellow Marines. The outcome was not favorable.

Eight days following that episode, Jason Dunham would succumb to the injuries he sustained in that selfless act. Fate would have that Dunham would become the first Marine since the Viet Nam War (as well as only the second Marine who'd served during

Operation Iraqi Freedom) to receive the Medal of Honor (post-humously, January 11th, 2007.)

The mother Veteran traveling with her son was intent on paying their respects to this hero and his family. Mama Vet was a published author and had decided to gift a copy of one of her Marine-themed novels to the Corporal's family, intending to leave it at the local post office with hopes that the Postmaster would oblige her request and forward it to Corporal Dunham's family. Mama Vet's son was an accomplished musician who had become accustomed to paying respects to different Marines and other soldiers who gave their all by way of playing hymns on his violin at their final resting sites.

Luck would have the Postmaster out to lunch when Mama Vet and her little boy arrived at the Scio post office. The two of them had already accomplished the first portion of their mission with a visit to Dunham's grave and were planning on returning to Elmira as soon as they were able to leave the book. They settled in to wait, sitting cross-legged on the floor in a corner of the newly renamed *Corporal Dunham Post Office*.

It wasn't long before a kindly, older, gentleman walked into the lobby. Apparently, he had observed their truck with its conspicuously out-of-state tags in the parking lot. Noticing Mama Vet and her son sitting there on the floor, he casually asked,

"Everything okay with you folks?"

Mama Vet assured the gentleman that all was well and that she and her son were simply waiting for the postmaster.

"That your truck out there in the parking lot?"

"Yes sir."

"You sure are a long way from home." He commented curiously.

Mama Vet stood up and automatically launched into explanation of the mission she and her son were anticipating to accomplish.

The man stood there a thoughtful moment, seemingly looking them up and down before speaking again. "The Dunham's live just a little bit down the road here." He casually suggested a turn at the bottom of a road in the direction he had pointed. "You might find them at the top of one of those hills out there. Try the house with the Marine flag out front." He was purposefully imprecise but had a smile in his eyes. "And here's my card."

Mama Vet and her son didn't wait a moment longer for the Postmaster as they decided to venture in the direction they had just been encouraged to travel. The gentleman was right. There was no mistaking which house it was. A Marine flag flowing proudly in the wind, they knew they had arrived at the right home. Shifting the truck into park, Mama and son prepared to go knock on the door.

A man on a riding mower had watched the truck make its way up the lengthy drive. He steered his way to the driveway and shut down the mower.

"Can I help you?"

Mama Vet did not know who the man was but immediately launched into explanation about how she and her son had stopped by Corporal Dunham's grave before finding their way to the Post Office and now the house.

"We left a book with him, and some flowers."

"And I played my violin." The little boy spoke up respectfully. "Mom said he is a hero and that it was good to come pay our respects." The little boy did not know who the man on the mower was either, but Mama Vet soon suspected his identity.

"Well I'm Dan, Dan Dunham. Jason is my son. It's too hot out here. Come on in." Mr. Dunham invited Mama Vet and her son into his home. Dan Dunham was immediately on the phone, his conversation succinct and to the point; "Deb, you need to come home a minute. There's a lady here I think you need to meet."

While they waited for Mrs. Dunham's arrival, Mr. Dunham began telling his visitors the story of Jason. Mama Vet had previously read the book, '*The Gift of Valor*' and had shared with her son the story about this Marine. At that moment, something dawned on the child.

"The flags, Mom. The red one was a Marine flag and the blue one with white stars was for the Medal of Honor." (The little boy had seen General Douglas MacArthur's Medal of Honor on a previous trip to Little Rock. He knew Corporal Dunham's story and had at that exact moment put everything together.)

Mrs. Dunham soon arrived, and Mr. Dunham explained who their company was. Deb Dunham was every bit as cordial as Dan and very willing to share the story of their son. The progression of the visit soon changed course to looking at and sharing the many treasures the Dunham's had gathered of their son. They told their visitors stories of Jason growing up as well as a more personal account of the story that became the book *Gift of Valor*.

As the visit was drawing to a close, Deb Dunham stood.

"Hold on a second." She disappeared into the next room. When she returned, she took the little boy's hand. "Your Mom can tell you what this is all about." She handed him a challenge coin. "And one for you too, Mom. Thank you both for what you've done for Jason."

The little boy accepted the coin and smiled. "I know what this is. You just 'coined' me." He closed his little hand on the coin. "I got 'coined' in Washington D.C. too. Thank you." He looked at his mom and declared, "We made another Marine mamas' heart happy."

Mama Vet thanked the Dunham's for their hospitality and she and her son started their return trip to Elmira. On the way out of Scio, they took notice they were driving on a stretch of highway that had been dedicated in Corporal Dunham's name. Mama Vet pur-posefully stopped to snap a photograph. The little boy looked at the sign and commented, "I paid respects to two Marines on this trip mom, and I made their mom's hearts a little less sad." Still grasping the challenge coin Deb Dunham had presented to him, the little boy sat back in his seat. "We have to come back here again."

-A Dash-

After life on earth is through, every person will have two dates attributed to them; the date they were born and the date they left this world. There is a whole lot of living that goes on between those dates; more for some, not enough for others. No matter who you are though, that time for everybody is represented by the same, small dash. What follows is but a portion of the dash belonging to Corporal Jason Lee Dunham, United States Marine.

From the Medal of Honor Citation as posted on the Iraqi Heroes Website:

> *"By his undaunted courage, intrepid fighting spirit and unwavering devotion for duty Corporal Dunham gallantly gave his life for country, thereby reflecting great credit upon himself and upholding the highest traditions of the Marine Corps and the United States Naval Service..."*

Post Script: On Saturday, November 13, 2010 at Port Everglades, Fort Lauderdale, Florida, the Navy commissioned an

Arleigh Burke Class guided missile destroyer named the USS Jason Dunham, (DDG-109).

> From an Interview October 10, 2014
>
> *In honor of the Marine Corps birthday, this month's issue of 'The Warrior Heart' chose to focus on stories, accounts, etc. about Marines. For the fact that Medal of Honor Recipient Jason L. Dunham's birthday also falls on this date, this reader asked to contribute an interview with the Corporals parents, Dan and Deb Dunham.*

It was an interview that took place exactly one month before the Marine Corporal's birthday. Though it had been over a year since their initial visit, Dan and Deb Dunham remembered Mama Vet and her musician and how they had chosen to remember their son. For people who did not serve with Jason Dunham or get to know him as a civilian, Deb Dunham described Jason as follows:

"He was always a prankster but was so goodhearted. Jason was the kind of guy who would champion anybody he felt needed him. He was very athletic, very competitive. He didn't necessarily play to win so much as play to challenge himself. So being how he was, school really wasn't Jason's first concern, but he knew if he wanted to play sports and compete, well, it was school policy that athletes had to maintain a certain grade point average." Deb Dunham paused. "And girls? Oh yes. Jason *always* had a girlfriend. An interesting thing about him though was that even with a breakup, he never left a relationship on bad terms."

Dunham's parents were asked to describe how and when it was that Jason aspired to be a Marine. Mrs. Dunham answered this question with relative ease.

"We found out that with four kids, we weren't going to be able to totally pay for all of them to attend college. By this point, Jason had already had enough of school and wasn't exactly the most interested in pursuing a college education, but he was interested in the military. At one time, he even talked about being a Navy Seal. Then, I don't know where exactly but he ran into a Marine recruiter. The next thing we knew, he came home and announced, '*I think I want to join the Marines.*' He signed into the delayed entry program the summer before his senior year." Deb Dunham paused. "Dan and I both had been discussing the value and benefits of the military with him on different occasions and apparently Jason took all that to heart."

When asked whether there was a Marine history in the family, Deb relayed the following.

"No, no Marine history really. My own dad did a stint in the Army, not a career man mind you, but he served. Dan was in the Air Force." Essentially, there was a great history of military service in the Dunham family, but the only Marine was Deb's sister-in-law's husband.

"Jason actually talked to him about joining."

"When Jason enlisted, there wasn't any threat of conflict but then 911 happened and Dan and I both grew concerned." Mrs. Dunham's voice was a little softer as she continued. "Before he deployed, Jason had called me at the school. He said, '*I have good news and some not so good news. The good news is that I'm going to be home for Christmas this year. The bad news is we're going to deploy.*'" Deb paused as she gathered her thoughts. "I had class going on when he called and one of his cousins was in my room. I handed the phone to his cousin while I stepped away to compose myself. After I came back, we just started talking about when he'd be home."

Mr. Dunham added his thoughts. "We were worried something was going to happen. So, Deb and I sat in the living room and started talking about it. I remember saying to her, 'I don't feel good about this because if something goes wrong, you know Jason's going to be right in the middle of it trying to protect his guys.' Which is, as you know, exactly what he did."

"We received a letter from him where he told us '*I might not be able to call you on the phone for a while.*' The last call we got from him sort of felt like good-bye. It wasn't a bad call, just a sense of..." Mr. Dunham's voice trailed off.

"The letter we received told us not to worry, that he would be home when the time was right. He had called to ask for the address of a girl whom he was close to... and told us not to worry. He'd be home... and he asked for chocolate chip cookies." Deb laughed a gentle laugh. "He was like, '*Where are the cookies?*'"

"When everything first happened, we didn't realize he had taken his Kevlar (helmet) off to cover the grenade. We learned that fact later. Apparently, Jason and the guys had been having a conversation just before this about whether or not a Kevlar could contain a grenade blast." Mr. Dunham paused thoughtfully. "Doing what he did, he saved his men. They had some shrapnel injuries, but there were no fatalities. Except for Jason."

The Dunham's were asked about their reactions when they were notified of Jason's passing. "When Jason died, we did not have to be notified. We were right there with him." Mr. Dunham spoke firmly. "We got the initial phone call at 1130 at night. They wouldn't talk to Deb so much because my name was all over his paper work. However, when they talked about what happened, they were very vague. At the initial call, we exchanged contact information and that was the start of our eight days of not sleeping...literally. We are kind of calm people, so our initial reaction was somewhat composed. We didn't get very excited at first because we didn't want to jump to any conclusions. I had told Deb to go try to get some rest, that I would stay up in case anybody else called. That was where our shock trauma started... and it still hasn't ended."

Mr. Dunham didn't take any pause as he continued to reveal the order of events. "As far as his passing, it happened eight days after the event. They flew him back to the states from Germany knowing he wasn't going to make it."

Mrs. Dunham added. "We each held one of Jason's hands and we held hands across him."

"There was one time he had made a comment that he didn't want to be vegetative. He didn't want to exist that way." Dan Dunham paused. "Don't think for a minute that moment wasn't the hardest thing in our lives." His voice grew silent after he referenced the decision to take their son off life-support.

Scio, New York is not a big city by any means. The Dunhams were asked to describe the town's reaction after learning what happened to their son.

"They were incredibly supportive through everything. After Jason died, we came back home to yellow ribbons, to them protecting our other children from the onslaught of press. They were very good. However, as with the course of time, well, there are some that still remember and constantly talk about Jason, and there are others…" Mrs. Dunham took an audibly deep breath. "-it's not every day for them like it is for us as parents. When Jason passed, they held his funeral in the school gymnasium; it was packed. There wasn't room…"

"So many people." Mrs. Dunham interjected.

"Life is never normal now. It's difficult. I mean, we still celebrate his birthday; we still hang his stocking at Christmas. We never talk about him in the past tense. Jason will *always* be our son, will *always* be with us. It still seems like only yesterday, it's *every* day for us and it always will be."

———

-Medal of Honor Park: Indianapolis, Indiana Trip-

This is a Medal of Honor Park on the White River that we've visited a number of times. It's especially nice to visit at night when all the glass panels are lit up.

We were all on our way to Indianapolis, Indiana to visit the Medal of Honor Memorial. What was going to turn into a crazy bit of an adventure happened when we got a flat tire in Muhlenberg County Kentucky down by the Green River ("-*Where Paradise lay…*" Thank you, John Prine.)

On our way up there from Arkansas, we researched information on many MOH recipients who were at rest in private cemeteries along the way. (Not all our heroes were laid to rest in National Cemeteries.) The route we were driving was going to take us across the state of Kentucky. Like always, we were traveling on a thin budget. The flat tire incident almost made us not get to go to Indianapolis, but something really neat happened instead.

We had just left Rosine, Kentucky and were making our way to Louisville. After the flat tire happened, Mom had to use our hotel money to buy a new tire at Walmart. We had a group discussion after we got done at the tire center where Mom let me and Derrick decide if we wanted to keep going to Indianapolis or turn around and go back home. We voted to keep going even though it meant we were all going to sleep in the car that night.

Mom said I could add a copy of this letter she sent to the police department to better explain things so here it is:

Dear Chief Throneberry,

My name is TM Fitzgerald. I'm sending this letter because of the thoughtful actions and kindness shown to me my son and his friend by one of your officers, Officer C-F. This necessitates my sharing a little bit of a story so please bear with me.

I am a veteran of the US Army. I am currently unemployed/between jobs/in a spot constantly but always manage to tuck a little bit of money away over the course of the year to take my extremely civic-minded son (and usually one of his little friends) on a trip of some sort for summer vacation. This year, we started a Medal of Honor Mission whereby on Medal of Honor Day (back in March), we officially began traveling to the gravesites of Medal of Honor recipients to pay respects. (We research each individual and read their citations and then the boys and I go visit their graves, say some words and travel to the next destination.)

On the weekend of June 13, we loaded the car and were making our way to Indianapolis to visit the Medal of Honor monument on the canal at Riverside Park. On the way, we had a bad experience with a flat tire, dealing with AAA while stranded on the roadside in Muhlenberg County...lots of issue there... but that is not why I am writing. This is about Officer F. and what happened later the same evening...

Due to the nature of what happened with the flat tire, my limited finances and the fiasco that was the beginning of our journey, by the time we made it up to Louisville, I was fighting to keep my eyes open. The boys were sound asleep in the backseat and I was not able to secure any lodging that evening. What I ended up doing was finding a vacant plaza parking lot behind the Stockyards Bank off Brownsboro and Newmarket Drive. (You see, we had two Medal of Honor recipients' graves to visit over at Zach Taylor Nat'l Cemetery the next morning anyway, so...)

I think it was a little after midnight (or later) when I sensed a car pulling up behind us. It was an officer with his light, checking us out. (I mean, I would have stopped to check and see what we were up to, too if I saw an out of state vehicle behind the bank at that hour of the morning.) It was your officer C.F. He asked what we were doing, and I explained the flat tire incident, the long drive and why I had two ten-year-old boys sleeping in my backseat. I ended my explanation by stating we had intention to visit the National Cemetery at daybreak, so I figured I'd just pull into the lot and catch some sleep.

Officer F. and I had a very detailed conversation actually. Given the circumstances and the fact I had two kids with me, he assured me it was okay for us to remain parked where we were then proceeded to do something that humbled me tremendously and restored my faith in humanity. Because of Officer F's kindness and generosity, he made this leg of our Medal of Honor Journey a very memorable success. What could have been a very tough situation and cause for me to shut our journey down before we got to Indianapolis was made a success directly because of the actions of Officer F.

Officer F. is a credit to your police force. You read and see negative things about law enforcement from all over the country and rarely are ever given to find out about selfless acts such as what Officer F, did. It may have seemed like no big deal but believe me, it was a TREMENDOUS deal for me and the boys. We will never forget Officer F. and how he became a part of our Medal of Honor Journey.

———

-Andrews Raiders and the Great Train Chase-

We had decided to go to Eastern Tennessee for part of our mission because we had learned that the very first recipients of the Medal of Honor were a group of men at rest there in Chattanooga. These guys were called *Andrews Raiders* and there is a very notable monument to them. They were a part of a Civil War event called *The Great Train Chase* and the monument is in the Chattanooga National Cemetery.

On July 16th, 2015 a Muslim gunman had opened fire in two separate attacks in Chattanooga on two Military recruiting centers. In his attacks, he killed four Marines and a Navy officer. While we were at the National cemetery on our mission, Marine Sergeant

David Wyatt, one of the Marines killed in the attacks, had just been laid to rest. We paid our respects to him, too.

A Memorial in Chattanooga, Tennessee

-One of My Texas Trips-

On one of my trips to Texas (one without Derrick) my dad, Grandpa and I went to the National Cemetery in Austin to pay respects to American Sniper Chris Kyle. (He is not a Medal of Honor recipient, but our visit was about paying respects.) His monument had not been put into place at the time we first went.

Austin, Texas

Visiting Austin Cemetery after Chris Kyle's monument was put in place. (That's my grandfather Mr. William Marshall Fitzgerald Sr. on the right.)

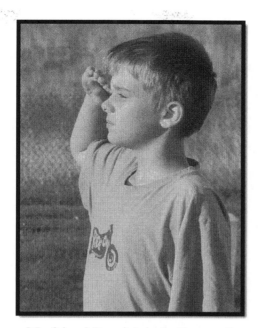

My friend Derrick in Indianapolis

Both of us in Indianapolis

Indiana

Leavenworth, Kansas

**Paying Respects in
Georgia**

-Gainesville, Texas- *"Medal of Honor Host City"*

At the Convention Center in Gainesville

At *Medal of Honor Park* in Gainesville, TX

Don Fitzgerald in his Boy Scout Class A's

Mr. Tom Kelly

Mr. Hiroshi Miyamura

Mr. Chuck Hagemeister

Mr. Michael Fitzmaurice

Mr. Don 'Doc' Ballard

Mr. Robert Modrzejewski

Mr. Walter J. Marm

Mr. Robert O'Malley

Mr. Herschel Williams

Mr. James Taylor

Mr. Robert Patterson

Mr. Melvin Morris

**Stopping in Elizaville, Kentucky to pay respects
to one of the Flag Raisers of Iwo Jima.**

SGT. MICHAEL STRANK
USMC

CPL. HARLON H. BLOCK
USMC

PFC. FRANKLIN R. SOUSLEY
USMCR

PFC. IRA H. HAYES
USMCR

PFC. RENE A. GAGNON
USMCR

PhM2. JOHN H. BRADLEY
USN

IN HONOR AND REMEMBRANCE
OF THE ABOVE FLAG RAISERS.

**Myself and Derrick
in Little Rock, Arkansas**

On one of my trips to San Antonio, TX

Ft. Benning, Georgia

My family and I were on our way to Atlanta, Georgia when we decided to take some time to drop farther south in the state and visit to Ft. Benning. This cemetery was located on post and so we had to get special permission to be allowed to go do what we do. There were a couple of funerals taking place while we were there, and I watched the flag. When a military funeral takes place, flags are lowered to half-mast. After the service, the flag is returned to the top of the pole. We saw services taking place on many occasions during our many missions.

Flags are half-mast during burials.

Full-mast when services are over.

The Rodney Davis Memorial

Rodney Davis, USMC

Seymour Terry, Little Rock Arkansas

Fitzgerald in Marietta, Georgia

-Missions of Honor 2019-
Parting Thoughts

It took Derrick and I about three years from the very beginning of these *Missions of Honor* to get to where we first considered our project complete. For myself though, I have to say that the mission hasn't really ended. I'll *always* be interested in learning about the heroes of our country and believe that anywhere I may travel in my future, I'll probably research information about Medal of Honor recipients who may be in my path. This turned into an actual mission instead of just a summer project to keep my friend and I busy over the months of summer break from school. I know I have learned a lot of things while working on this for so many years.

I'm glad my friend could be a part of so much of these travels. It made things more interesting instead of me doing all this by myself. I also included my Mom in this book because she was the one who had to drive us everywhere and she helped me get this book published. There were also a few times when other people joined in and learned about our heroes as well like my Grandma and Grandpa Fitzgerald, and my Aunt Stacey.

Our *Missions of Honor* has been something I will never forget. I learned so many things while we researched these men and as we traveled to all the different places we had to go. My friend had never been to *Arlington National Cemetery,* so he got to travel with us there and to the WWII Museum in New Orleans, too. In the summer of our second year doing this, Derrick even traveled with us to Scio, New York where mom and I originally began this project. I thought it was awesome how we all sort of ended the official mission in the same place Mom and I started it years before.

We had stories connected to so many of these heroes. For example, when I went to Rosine, Kentucky, I discovered that one of our MOH recipients (Wesley Phelps) was laid to rest only a few graves away from Bluegrass Legend Bill Monroe. Being a Bluegrass Musician myself, I had also visited the Monroe Homestead at Jerusalem Ridge which was just up the road. It seemed we traveled the Bluegrass Highway quite a bit on our trips.

We were able to return to Gainesville, Texas for a third year in a row to continue the *Missions of Honor* we had started. I was not able to put any pictures from that trip into this project though because I wanted to have copies of this book ready to take to Texas with me to share with our Medal of Honor Heroes. I still had a lot of writing to do and edits to make and had to make sure everything was just right before I made all of this into a literal book.

Besides being a Veteran of the United States Army, my mom was already a published author who helps fellow Veterans in whatever ways she can. She thinks our country should do more to honor people who have served and does whatever she can do to encourage others to do the same. Sometimes it isn't just Veterans she helps but their moms and families as well. This book is about a different mission than all of that, though. It's about honoring and remembering guys who gave their best and who gave their all.

—

-In Conclusion-

My name is TM Fitzgerald. I am a very proud Veteran and self-appointed Veteran's advocate. However, above all else, I am Mom. Many things in this world are out of anyone's control but there are two things specifically that each of us *can* manage. We can *teach,* and we can *encourage.* These actions go hand in hand and no money or special tools are required. There only has to be *desire.* That's what *this* project was all about.

It was rather fortuitous that while partaking in this ambitious mission with the boys that we learned about the *Medal of Honor Foundation's Character Development Program* and subsequently the *Medal of Honor Host City* of Gainesville, Texas. I wanted to teach and share with the two young men featured in this book (my son and his friend) everything that I could about the importance of respect, remembrance and gratitude. I taught them to look at the larger picture, at things greater than us all and how everything is connected.

For many kids today (and adults), when the words '*Medal of Honor*' are mentioned, thoughts immediately turn to nothing more than an apparently popular video game. Kids don't know about this country's highest military honor much less of the actions partaken by individuals who have received the honor. That, coupled with Common Core curriculum forced into schools of today made me seek out something greater to share with these two kids. I wanted to give them something to remember, to be proud of when they looked back at this time in their lives. I wanted to share a sense of pride and patriotism, to teach them that valor and heroism are honorable traits to possess.

Of course, the first year we went to Gainesville, Texas none of us knew what to expect. It was an amazing experience from watching the parade with hundreds of other people all the way up to meeting many Medal of Honor Recipients all in one place at one time. (We immediately planned to return the following year.)

As the year progressed, we carried on with our expanded mission, researching and learning about other Medal of Honor Recipients and counting down the days until we would return. April rolled back around, and we hit the road for our much-anticipated trip. The boys were more comfortable and no less excited to be meeting with such an incredible group of heroes once again. (However, it would be the third year that things really hit home.)

I knew I'd accomplished what I had intended with introducing the kids to this project when my son and Derrick started being able to quote opening sentences from Medal of Honor Citations. They understood the magnitude of the actions of these men. It was for this reason I became saddened, too. You must wonder why. When I would share the amazing accomplishments of these two young men with others, more times than not I found myself on the receiving end of some rather defensive responses from other adults. As much as that made me bristle, I never apologized for teaching these kids to care, to be patriotic or have pride in their country. More people should aspire to do as much.

Why did I encourage the continuation of such a project? That answer has already been explained, but at the same time, folks should know something else. Amazing things happened all through the years we carried on in this journey.

This journey, or *mission* as the boys took to calling it was not something set into stone. By that I mean to say we never followed any clearly defined methodology, there were no exact steps to follow and we certainly had no prior experience on which to base our path. This *Missions of Honor* project simply evolved. No two trips were exactly alike.

While many people from the outside looking in felt to express how odd it was (or in the very least, peculiar) that I traveled to such lengths to take these two young men to so many places, cemeteries of all locations, I never looked at our actions from such a perspective.

These *Missions of Honor* were about history. This experience was about learning appreciation of our own country, of the rights and freedoms we enjoy here and at what cost they remain ours. Too many people take life in America for granted and any attempt to remind them of those costs are for the most part met with disinterest and defensive rejoinders.

When two young men don't just show but can *prove* their genuine knowledge and interest in things that many grown men have no knowledge of or desire to learn about? It speaks volumes about the character of all involved.

Taking these two young men from the confines of their comfort zones and showing them that there's more to the world than what sits just outside the front door? Quite costly, indeed especially considering how up until our third trip to Gainesville, Texas we accomplished everything on this *Missions of Honor* project with funds out of my own pocket. (I must take pause to express *tremendous* gratitude to Mr. Richard Norris, fellow Veteran and Veteran's Advocate for all that he has done for me over the past decade and helping me continue the missions these kids started. Without him, this project would not have progressed as far as the kids were able to take it.)

Researching scores of men deemed heroes and learning about the wars and conflicts they were each involved in? Time-consuming, to say the least. Meeting many of this country's living Medal of Honor Recipients and getting to shake their hands? *Priceless*. Truly priceless. I know two young men who would absolutely agree.

———

The following pages were intentionally left blank for the Medal of Honor City Event, Gainesville, Texas 2019.

Autograph:

Autograph:

Autograph:

Autograph:

Autograph:

Autograph:

Autograph:

Autograph:

Autograph:

Autograph:

Autograph:

Autograph:

Autograph:

Autograph:

Autograph:

Autograph:

Autograph:

Autograph:

Autograph:

Autograph:

Autograph:

Autograph:

Autograph:

Autograph:

Autograph:

Autograph:

Autograph:

Autograph:

-List of Medal of Honor Recipients Respects Were Paid To-

The following is a list of the nearly 200 men that I (and many with Derrick) traveled and paid my respects to or studied on and learned about over a period of four years. Their names are shown in no particular order.

Michal P. Murphy	Tomb of the Unknowns
Audie L. Murphy	Franklin W. Lutes
Douglas Macarthur	Richard J. Curran
Jason L. Dunham	Timothy O'Donoghue
Calvary Young	Warren Carman
Arthur Macarthur	William W. Winegar
John Poppe	George Grueb
George Lloyd	John Kiggins
William Windrich	George Ladd
Charles P. Murray, Jr.	Charles Morse
Alan L. Eggers	James Roberts
John Basilone	Robert Pinn
Clyde Thomason	William Richardson
William G. Walsh	George Kelley
Larry Smedley	Franklin Sousley

Andrews Raiders

William H. Howe

Freeman Gill

Charles J. Bibber

James Bensen

Francis M. McMillen

Isaac Harrison Carman

Howell Burr Treat

Charles Porter Mattocks

Sidney Warren Thaxter

Charles Day

Russell C. Elliot

Edward W. Hathaway

James Madison Burns

Stephen Thomas

Thomas Stanton

Michael Walsh

George Bradley

Marcus Aurelius Hanna

John Henry Pruit II

Fitz Lee

Mary Edwards Walker

Nicholas Oresko

John William Finn

Thomas Ward Custer

William E. Hall

Harry Bell

Lehmann Hinemann

John Kyle

Fitz Lee

Edward Pengally

Joseph Robinson

Albert D. Sale

Jacob Widner

Maurice Britt

Jack Williams

Fred Henry McGuire

Orion P. Howe

Patrick Henry Pentzer

Harrison Collins

James H. Robinson

Walter Singleton

Joseph Adkison

Edgar Lloyd

George Taylor Johnson	Raymond Cooley
James Gardner	Desmond Doss
Seymour Terry	Ray E. Duke
John Kennedy	William Zion
Joshua Hartzog	David R. Ray
David Barkley	Milo Lambert
Solon D. Neal	Alvin C. York
Wesley Phelps	Oliver Rood
John Squires	John H. Willis
Willie Sandlin	William F. Lyle
Perry Wilkes	Charles P. Cantrell
James Archer	Seth Weld
Thomas Box	Hershel Williams
Gerry Kisters	Bennie Adkins
Jacob Johnson	Thomas Norris
Charles Brouse	Jake Lindsay
Nick Bacon	Earle D. Gregory
Clarence B. Craft	Ross Franklin
Daniel Edwards	William Marland
M. Waldo Hatler	Raymond G. Davis
Wilson D. Watson	Lee H. Phillips
Bolden Harrison	Samuel Fuqua

Dennis Buckley

Peter Johnson

William J. Bordelon

Lucian Adams

Roy Benavidez

Richard Rocco

Jose Lopez

Cleto Rodriguez

John Carr

Milton A. Lee

George W. Smth

Lewis Warrington

John J. Given

James Nash

Jimmie E. Howard

Frederick Deetline

Henry Falcot

James E. Robinson Jr

John Harrington

Simon Suhler

John N. Reese

Billy Bowlegs

Tony K. Burris

Henry A. McMasters

William H. Barnes

James M. Logan

William Harrel

William DeArmond

David H. McNerney

Joseph C. Rodriguez

Robert Edward Galer

George Herman O'Brian

Robert Burton Nett

Donald R. Johnston

Edward Schowalter, Jr.

Luther H, Story

James B. Wiley

Rodney Maxwell Davis

Manuel Flores

James Lamar Stone

Russell Steindam

Neel Kearby

Turney W. Leonard

Martin Schubert

Michael Blassie

Lorenzo Immel

Francis Brownell

Ralph Cheli

Lorenzo Stokes

Bruce VanVoorhies

Donald Pucket

George Hobday

Wilson Brown

Ira C. Wellborn

John New

George 'Bud' Day

Clifford Simmons

Clyde Lassen

Lloyd Hughes, Jr

Timothy Spillane

Troy A. McGill

James E. Karnes

Edward R. Talley

Mitchell W. Stout

Ernest Childers

John R. Crews

Harold L. Turner

Jack Montgomery

Stephen Pless

-END-

Made in the USA
Columbia, SC
20 October 2022

69761262R10080